Christmas Cookie Walk Favorites
Amana Church Society

Copyright © 2020
Amana Church Society
Box 103
Middle Amana, Iowa
52307

ISBN 978-0-9764491-2-6

Cover Design by Erin Wilding

Printing by Pella Printing Co., Pella, Iowa

The Amana Church Society

The Amana Church was established in Germany in 1714 and was first known as "the Community of True Inspiration." Over a dozen members of the 18th and 19th century church community, men and women, were inspired by the Holy Spirit to speak out for Christ. Advocating a simple form of worship that allows time for silent reflection and prayer, the Amana Church encourages spirit-filled worship. Today the Amana Church serves its community as a peaceful haven of worship and fellowship.

Our Christmas Cookie Walk

The Amana Church Cookie Walk began in 1991 as a way to raise money to support youth activities (Sunday School, Youth Group, and Vacation Bible School) and continues to provide funds for youth activities today. As soon as the Thanksgiving holiday is over, attention turns to the thousands of cookies to be baked and candies to be made before the first weekend of December. Bakers pull out family cookie recipes, stock their pantries with flour and sugar, and warm their ovens in preparation for the annual event. It is a time of year when friends and family gather in the kitchen to bake delicious treats and begin the joy-filled Christmas season.

Why a New Edition?

There are several reasons for this edition of *Christmas Cookie Walk Favorites*. First, it is in recognition of the 25 years since the original *Christmas Cookie Walk Collection* was published. Second, it is a celebration of the wonderful tradition that has enabled the Amana Church to reach out to youth in the community. Third, there have been many requests over the years for additional copies or editions of the original recipe book. Fourth, many new cookies have debuted and become "regulars" at the cookie walk and deserve to be included in this collection of our favorites! And most importantly, it is an additional means by which to support youth at the Amana Church with all proceeds directly supporting youth activities.

Thank You!

Thank you to all of the cookie bakers and candy makers who have contributed to the cookie walk during the last 30 years. Many of our favorite recipes were originally provided by bakers who have since passed away and we carry on baking in their honor. Many thanks to those who contributed recipes to this collection and of course, to our patrons who support the Amana Church youth activities by buying our cookies during the Christmas season!

The Amana Church Cookie Walk Committee
 and the Cookbook Committee

Recipes from the bakers and candy makers of the Amana Church Cookie Walk

To order another copy of this book please go to:
Amanachurch.com

"Taste and see that the Lord is good. . ."
Psalm 34:8

Table of Contents

Cookies

Tante's Sour Cream Cookies

2 ½ cups cake flour
1 teaspoon nutmeg
¼ teaspoon baking soda
2 teaspoons baking powder
½ cup butter
1 cup brown sugar, firmly packed
1 egg
2 tablespoons grated orange rind
1 cup chopped pecans
½ cup sour cream

Combine flour, nutmeg, baking soda and baking powder; set aside. Cream butter and brown sugar until fluffy. Add egg, orange rind and chopped nuts. Stir in flour mixture alternating with sour cream. Blend. Drop by rounded spoonfuls onto a greased baking sheet. Bake at 375 degrees for about 10 to 12 minutes.
Once cool, dust with powdered sugar or glaze with vanilla icing.

Yield: 5 to 6 dozen

Emilie Wendler Steele

Nutmeg Sugar Crisps

1 cup butter (2 sticks), softened
¾ cup granulated sugar
½ cup confectioners' sugar
1 egg, beaten
1 teaspoon vanilla extract
2 ½ cups all purpose flour
½ teaspoon baking soda
½ teaspoon cream of tartar
½ teaspoon ground nutmeg
1/8 teaspoon salt

In a mixing bowl, cream butter and sugars. Beat in egg and vanilla; mix well. Combine flour, baking soda, cream of tartar, nutmeg and salt; add to the creamed mixture and mix well. Refrigerate 1 hour. Shape dough into ¾ inch balls; place 2 inches apart on greased baking sheets. Flatten with a glass dipped in granulated sugar. Bake at 350 degrees for 10 to 12 minutes or until lightly browned.

Yield: 6 dozen

Donna Trumpold

Chocolate Truffle Cookies

2 cups semi-sweet chocolate morsels – divided
4 ounces unsweetened chocolate, cut into pieces
1/3 cup butter, cut into pieces
1 cup granulated sugar
3 large eggs
1 ½ teaspoons vanilla extract
½ cup all purpose flour
2 tablespoons baking cocoa
¼ teaspoon baking powder
¼ teaspoon salt
confectioners' sugar

In a microwave oven, melt 1 cup chocolate morsels, unsweetened chocolate and butter; stir until smooth. Cool 10 minutes. In a large bowl, beat sugar and eggs 2 minutes. Beat in chocolate mixture and vanilla. In another bowl, whisk flour, cocoa, baking powder and salt; gradually beat into the chocolate mixture. Stir in the remaining chocolate chips. Refrigerate, covered, at least 3 hours, until firm enough to handle. Preheat oven to 350 degrees. With lightly floured hands, shape the dough into 1-inch balls; Place 2 inches apart on ungreased baking sheets. Bake at 350 degrees 10 – 12 minutes until lightly puffed and set. Cool on baking sheets 3 minutes. Remove to wire racks to cool. Dust with confectioners' sugar.

Yield: 4 dozen

Swedish Almond Cookies

½ cup butter
1 cup granulated sugar
1 egg
½ teaspoon almond extract
1 ¾ cup all purpose flour

2 teaspoons baking powder
¼ teaspoon salt
2 tablespoons milk
½ cup sliced almonds

Icing:
1 cup confectioners' sugar
¼ teaspoon almond extract

¼ cup milk

Line two cookie sheets with parchment paper. Preheat oven to 325 degrees. In a medium bowl, cream butter and sugar. Add egg and almond extract. Beat until fluffy. Stir in flour, baking powder and salt. Mix well. Divide dough into 4 parts. Roll each part into a log about 12 inches long. Place 2 logs on a cookie sheet about 4 inches apart. Flatten each roll by hand until it is about 3 inches wide. Brush flattened dough with milk and sprinkle with sliced almonds. Bake at 325 degrees for 12 to 15 minutes until edges are slightly browned. While cookies are still warm, cut them crosswise at a diagonal into slices about 1-inch wide. Allow cookies to cool before drizzling with almond icing. Almond icing: Beat together confectioners' sugar, almond extract and milk until smooth.

Yield: 5 to 6 dozen

Elly Hoehnle

Hazelnut Logs

1 cup butter, softened
¾ cup brown sugar, firmly packed
1 tablespoon Frangelico liqueur
2 1/2 cups all purpose flour
¼ teaspoon salt
1 1/2 cups finely chopped hazelnuts

Cream butter and brown sugar in a large bowl until light and fluffy. Beat in Frangelico liqueur. In a separate bowl, mix flour and salt; gradually beat into creamed mixture. Place hazelnuts in a small bowl. On a lightly floured surface, roll about ½ cupfuls of dough into ½-inch thick ropes. Cut ropes into 2-inch-long pieces. Roll pieces in the hazelnuts to coat. Place pieces about 1-inch apart on ungreased baking sheets. Bake at 375 degrees for 8-10 minutes or until light brown. Remove to wire racks to cool.

Betsy Momany

Chocolate Cookies

1 cup (6 ounces) chocolate morsels
6 ounces bittersweet chocolate, broken into large pieces
   (Suggestion: use Lindt bittersweet or Godiva dark)
1 ½ cups all purpose flour
1/3 cup unsweetened cocoa
1 ½ tablespoon baking powder
½ teaspoon salt
½ cup butter – divided
¾ cup brown sugar, firmly packed
¾ cup granulated sugar
3 eggs
1 ½ tablespoons vanilla

In a double boiler, melt chocolate morsels, bittersweet chocolate and 4 tablespoons butter. Then remove from heat to cool. Sift together flour, cocoa, baking powder and salt; set aside In a large bowl, beat 4 tablespoons butter with sugars until it looks like wet sand; add eggs and vanilla. Add cooled chocolate mixture and sifted dry ingredients. Mix until no flour appears. Cover bowl and refrigerate for 25 minutes. Drop by rounded teaspoonsful on to ungreased cookies sheets. Bake cookies at 350 degrees, 9 to 11 minutes, until cookies have puffed and flattened. Do not overbake.

Katie Berger

Butterscotch Morsels

1 cup margarine
1 cup granulated sugar
1 cup brown sugar, firmly packed
1 egg
1 teaspoon vanilla
4 ½ cups all purpose flour
1 cup sour cream
1 teaspoon baking powder
½ teaspoon baking soda
1 12 ounce bag butterscotch morsels

Cream margarine and sugars. Blend in egg, vanilla and soda. Alternately add flour and sour cream, putting baking powder into the last cup of flour. Stir in butterscotch morsels. Drop by rounded spoonfuls onto cookie sheets.
Bake at 375 degrees for 8 to 10 minutes

Yield: 5 to 6 dozen

Shirley Reihman

White Chocolate Cranberry Cookies

1/3 cup butter, softened
½ cup brown sugar, firmly packed
1/3 cup granulated sugar
1 egg
1 teaspoon vanilla extract
1 ½ cups all purpose flour
½ teaspoon salt
½ teaspoon baking soda
¾ cup dried cranberries
½ cup vanilla or white chocolate morsels

In a large mixing bowl, beat butter and sugars until crumbly, about 2 minutes. Beat in egg and vanilla. Combine flour, salt and baking soda; gradually add to butter mixture and mix well. Stir in cranberries and morsels. Drop by rounded tablespoonfuls 2 inches apart onto cookie sheets coated with nonstick cooking spray.
Bake at 375 degrees for 8 to 10 minutes or until lightly browned.
Cool for 1 minute before removing to wire cooling racks.

Yield: 2 dozen

Chocolate Nut Revels

1 cup (6 ounces) semi-sweet chocolate morsels
1 cup pecans, chopped
1 cup butter
2/3 cup granulated sugar
¼ teaspoon salt
1 teaspoon vanilla extract
2 cups sifted all purpose flour

Melt chocolate chips in double boiler or microwave oven. Stir in chopped pecans. Set aside. Cream butter and sugar well; stir in salt and vanilla. Gradually blend in flour. Add melted chocolate and nuts; stir with fork just enough to revel (marble) chocolate into white batter. Drop by teaspoonfuls onto ungreased cookie sheets.
Flatten to ¼-inch thickness using a glass, greased and dipped into sugar.
Bake at 350 degrees for 10 to 12 minutes.

Yield: 4 dozen

Amy Jacobson

Cookies that Bake While You Sleep

2 egg whites
¼ teaspoon salt
¼ teaspoon cream of tartar
2/3 cup granulated sugar
1 teaspoon vanilla extract
¼ teaspoon almond extract
1 cup chopped pecans
¾ cup miniature chocolate morsels

Preheat oven to 350 degrees.
Beat egg white until very frothy. Add salt and cream of tartar as if making meringue.
When almost stiff, gradually add sugar. Continue beating until stiff. Add vanilla and
almond extract. Fold in pecans and mini-chocolate morsels.
Drop by teaspoonfuls onto two, foil lined cookie sheets. Place cookie sheets in oven
and turn off the heat. Leave overnight in oven. Do not open the oven to peek!

Yield: 4 dozen

Amy Jacobson

Famous Oatmeal Cookies

¾ cup vegetable shortening
1 cup brown sugar, firmly packed
½ cup granulated sugar
1 egg
¼ cup water
1 teaspoon vanilla extract
1 cup all purpose flour
1 teaspoon salt
½ teaspoon baking soda
3 cups oatmeal

Cream shortening and sugars, add egg, water and vanilla. Sift together flour, salt and baking soda. Stir sifted ingredients into batter. Stir in oatmeal. Drop by teaspoonfuls on greased cookie sheet. Bake at 350 degrees for 8 to 12 minutes.

Yield: 5 dozen

Marie Stumpff

Peppermint Candy Cane Cookies

1 ½ cups butter, softened
2 cups granulated sugar
2 eggs
1 ½ teaspoons peppermint extract
1 teaspoon vanilla extract
4 ½ cups all purpose flour
Red food coloring

In large bowl, cream butter and sugar. Beat in egg. Stir in peppermint and vanilla.
Gradually stir in flour. Divide the dough in half. Color one half with red food coloring.
Refrigerate overnight. Roll out a tablespoon of red dough and same amount of plain
dough until they are 6 inches long. Twist them together into a candy cane. Pinch the
ends. Curl top half to make candy cane shape. Repeat.
Bake on an UNGREASED cookie sheet for 8 to 10 minutes or until set – not brown.

Yield: 4 dozen

Mary Burgher

Drop Cookies

4 eggs
1 pound brown sugar (2 ¼ cups firmly packed)
2 tablespoons melted butter
1 teaspoon baking soda
1 pound all purpose flour (3 1/3 cups)

Cream butter, sugar and eggs. Sift together flour and baking soda;
add to creamed mixture. Drop by teaspoonfuls on greased cookie sheets.
Bake at 350 degrees for about 6 minutes.
Dough can be made ahead and refrigerated before baking.

Note: This is a traditional Amana Colony recipe. A simple, basic recipe, you may create variations by adding 2/3 cup ground nuts, 2/3 cup raisins or 2/3 cup flaked coconut to the batter.

Marie Stumpff

Tante's Snowballs with a Twist

¾ cup butter, softened
½ cup granulated sugar
1 egg
2 teaspoons vanilla extract

2 cups all purpose flour
½ teaspoon salt
1 cup finely chopped walnuts or pecans
1 cup mini chocolate morsels

Confectioners' sugar

In a bowl, cream butter and sugar. Add egg and vanilla, blend well. Combine flour and salt and stir into creamed mixture. Fold in nuts and chocolate chips. Roll into 1 inch balls. Place on ungreased baking sheets. Bake at 350 degrees for 15 to 18 minutes. Cool cookies slightly then roll in powdered sugar.

Variation: for a peppermint twist, finely crush a dozen Altoid brand peppermints and add to the confectioners' sugar before you roll the cookies.

Yield: 4 dozen

Note: *Tante* is German for aunt. This is a traditional Amana Colony recipe that's been given a modern twist with the addition of nuts, chocolate and peppermint.

Emilie Hoppe

Snowballs

1 cup butter
½ cup confectioners' sugar
¼ teaspoon salt
1 teaspoon vanilla extract
2 ¼ cups all purpose flour

confectioners' sugar

Preheat oven to 350 degrees. Cream butter, confectioners' sugar and vanilla. Blend in flour and salt. Roll about 1 tablespoon dough into balls and place on ungreased cookie sheet. Bake at 350 degrees for 15 minutes. Do not allow cookies to brown. While cookies are still hot, roll in confectioners' sugar. After cookies are cool, roll them in confectioners' sugar again.

Note: Also known as Tea Cakes or Mexican Wedding Cakes, these are a favorite in many Amana homes.

Verona Schinnerling and Susanna Hahn

Cranberry Orange Drops

1 cup granulated sugar
½ cup brown sugar, firmly packed
1 cup butter, softened
2 heaping tablespoons finely grated orange peel
2 tablespoons fresh-squeezed orange juice
2 cups dried cranberries, chopped into small pieces

1 egg
2 ½ cups all purpose flour
½ teaspoons baking soda
½ teaspoon salt
½ cup pecans, chopped

Orange glaze:

2 cups confectioners' sugar
1 tablespoon butter, melted

1 teaspoon finely grated orange peel
3 tablespoons orange juice

Preheat oven to 375 degrees. In a large mixing bowl, using an electric mixer, cream sugars and butter, blend in orange peel, orange juice and egg. Stir in flour, baking soda and salt. With spoon, stir in cranberries and nuts. Drop by rounded tablespoonfuls about 2 inches apart onto ungreased cookie sheets (best to line with parchment paper). Bake 12 to 14 minutes until light brown. Remove from cookie sheet and allow to cool completely.

Glaze: beat together sugar, butter, orange peel and juice. If glaze is too stiff to drizzle, add a drop or two of milk. Drizzle on cookies.

Yield: 4 to 5 dozen

Emilie Hoppe

Christmas Gems

1 cup granulated sugar
1 ½ cup all purpose flour
1 teaspoon cinnamon
1 teaspoon ground cloves
2/3 cup butter or margarine
2 eggs

1 cup boiling water
1 teaspoon baking soda
1 pound pecans or walnuts, chopped
1 pound raisins
1 pound dates, chopped
Small foil candy/dessert cups

You will need mini muffin tins and mini baking cup liners.
Combine sugar, flour, cinnamon and clove.
In a second bowl, beat together butter, eggs, boiling water and baking soda.
Blend dry and liquid ingredients. Fold in nuts, raisins and dates. Preheat oven to 400 degrees. Spoon batter into mini muffin tins lined with foil or paper cup liners.
Bake at 400 degrees for 15 minutes.

Yield: 8 to 10 dozen

Susan Hollrah

Lebkuchen
The South Amana Recipe

2 cups honey
1 cup plus 3 tablespoons brown sugar, firmly packed
1/8 teaspoon allspice
1/8 teaspoon cinnamon
1 1/2 teaspoons baking soda
Vanilla frosting

1/8 cup whiskey
2 eggs
4 3/4 cups all purpose flour, sifted
1/4 pound hickory or walnuts, ground (1 ½ cups)
½ cup candied citron, finely minced

In a heavy bottomed saucepan on medium-low heat, heat the honey, stirring in the brown sugar. When warm, add allspice and cinnamon. Stir baking soda in whiskey until dissolved.

In a very large mixing bowl, combine honey mixture and whiskey. Slowly beat in eggs and flour. Blend in nuts and citron. Stir until batter is formed. Cover and refrigerate at least overnight.

On a board or in the bowl, use your hands to knead dough. Knead well for at least 10 minutes until dough achieves a lighter quality. Do not rush this step – kneading is important. Preheat oven to 325 degrees. On a lightly floured board, cut a chunk of dough and roll out into a long, 1 inch thick rope. Cut rope into 2 or 3 inch long pieces. Place pieces on greased baking

sheet. Bake at 325 degrees about 10 to 12 minutes or until a deep golden color. Cookies should be dark gold in color, oval in shape and about ½ inch thick. When completely cool, frost with white vanilla icing.

Note: If you like, spice it up and increase the amount of cinnamon and allspice to ½ teaspoon. Lebkuchen is a traditional Amana Christmas cookie recipe and has little in common with the German cookie of the same name. There are a half dozen or more variations of this recipe in the Colonies. This recipe is from the village of South Amana and the Berger family.

Yield: 5 dozen

Henrietta B. Berger

Maple Oatmeal Cookies

1 cup butter, softened
¾ cup granulated sugar
¾ cup brown sugar, firmly packed
2 large eggs
1 teaspoon maple flavoring
2 cups all purpose flour
1 cup oatmeal
1 teaspoon baking soda
1 teaspoon salt
½ cup chopped pecans or English walnuts

Glaze:
1/3 cup butter
1 ¾ cup confectioners' sugar
1/3 cup maple syrup
¼ teaspoon maple flavoring

Preheat oven to 350 degrees. Cream butter and sugars in a large bowl until fluffy. Stir in egg and maple flavoring. In another bowl, combine flour, oatmeal, baking soda and salt. Beat into creamed mixture. Stir in nuts. (If you feel this is too dry, add a dash of milk. Batter should be fairly stiff) Drop by rounded tablespoonfuls on greased or parchment paper covered baking sheets. Bake 10 to 12 minutes or until golden. Cool on pans. Glaze cookies while on the pans to minimize clean up.

To make the glaze: In a saucepan, melt butter over medium heat. Remove from heat; then gradually beat in confectioners' sugar, syrup and maple flavoring until smooth. Drizzle over cookies. Let dry before storing. Best to store between layers of waxed paper.

Rachel Ehrman

Ice Box Cookies – Two Ways

1 cup butter
1 cup vegetable shortening
2 cups brown sugar, firmly packed
2 cups granulated sugar
4 eggs
2 teaspoons baking soda

3 cups all purpose flour
3 cups quick cook oatmeal
2 teaspoons vanilla extract
1 cup walnuts or pecans, chopped
1 cup shredded coconut

Combine butter, shortening and sugars until fluffy. Add eggs. Add flour and baking soda then oatmeal and vanilla to form a stiff dough. Use your hands to knead or a wooden spoon to work dough. Divide dough in half. Add chopped nuts to one half and coconut to the other half. Work nuts through dough. Shape dough into long rolls or logs. Wrap in waxed paper. Chill overnight.

Preheat oven to 350 degrees. Line baking sheets with parchment paper. I like to form the nut cookies into rectangles, so I flatten the sides of the roll before cutting (that's the way Oma did it). Using a very sharp knife, slice into 1/3 inch thick slices, rotating the log or roll as you cut it. Place on cookie sheets about 2 inches apart.

Bake 13 to 15 minutes (a minute longer if the dough is frozen) until they are pale golden. Allow to cool.

Marie Ruedy

Fudge Topped Shortbread

Shortbread:
1 cup butter
¾ cup sifted confectioners' sugar
1/8 teaspoon salt
2 cups all purpose flour
1 teaspoon vanilla extract

Fudge frosting:
2 tablespoons butter
2 oz (2 squares) semi-sweet baking chocolate
½ cup granulated sugar
1/3 cup whipping cream or ¼ cup evaporated milk

Shortbread:
In a mixing bowl, combine butter, confectioners' sugar and salt; beat with an electric mixer on medium speed until combined. Beat in flour and vanilla until combined (dough should be stiff). Form balls using approximately 1 tablespoon of dough for each cookie. Place one inch apart on an ungreased cookie sheet. Bake at 300 degrees for 18 to 20 minutes or until the edges are lightly browned. Cool cookies completely before topping with fudge frosting.

Fudge frosting:
In a small, heavy saucepan, melt the butter and chocolate over low heat. Stir in the sugar and whipping cream or evaporated milk. Cook and stir until the mixture begins to bubble - boil for 1 minute. Remove from heat. Beat with an electric mixer on medium speed about 4 to 5 minutes until frosting is thick enough to stick to cookie.

Fudge Topped Shortbread *(continued from pg 27)*

Dip the top of each cooked cookie into the frosting. (If frosting gets too hard, add a few more drops of whipping cream or evaporated milk.) If desired, sprinkle with chopped nuts. Let stand until frosting is firm.

Yield: 3 dozen

Kim Zuber

Snowflake Waffle Cookies

½ cup butter
½ cup granulated sugar
3 eggs
1 cup all purpose flour, sifted
1 teaspoon baking powder

¾ teaspoon baking soda
¼ teaspoon salt
2 heaping tablespoons grated orange rind
¼ cups pecans, finely chopped

Cream butter and sugars. Beat until fluffy.
Add eggs, one by one, beating after each egg.
In a second bowl, combine flour, baking powder, baking soda and salt. Stir flour mixture into batter and combine well. Fold in orange rind and nuts.
Heat waffle iron per instructions. Drop batter by tablespoon on heated waffle iron.
Leave space between each spoonful. (Makes about a 2 inch diameter cookie.)
Cool on wire rack. When completely cool, dust with confectioners' sugar.

Pfeffernüsse

1 egg
¼ cup butter, melted
1 cup brown sugar, packed
¼ cup honey
2 1/4 cups all purpose flour
1/4 teaspoon baking soda
1/4 teaspoon ground cloves

1/2 teaspoon ground cinnamon
1/2 teaspoon ground nutmeg
1/4 teaspoon cardamon
1/8 teaspoon ground black pepper
1 tablespoon fresh orange zest
1/2 cup walnuts, finely chopped or ground
1 cup confectioners' sugar

In a large bowl, cream egg, melted butter, brown sugar and honey. Combine flour, baking soda, spices, black pepper and ground nuts. Gradually blend into the creamed egg and sugar mixture beating well. Stir in grated orange zest. Cover bowl. Refrigerate for at least 8 hours.

Preheat oven to 350 degrees. Roll dough into 1-inch balls. Place on ungreased cookie sheets and bake in 350 degree oven about 13 minutes or until light brown and slight cracks form on top. While still warm, roll cookies in confectioners' sugar. In Amana kitchens this traditional German spice cookie is often made with ground walnuts.

Traditional Amana Colony Recipe

Caramel Pecan Turtles

Cookie base:

1 cup vegetable shortening
1 ½ cups granulated sugar
½ cup brown sugar, firmly packed
2 tablespoons milk
3 eggs

1 teaspoon vanilla extract
4 to 5 cups all purpose flour
1 ½ cups baking soda
1 ½ teaspoon cream of tartar
1 teaspoon salt

Toppings:
28 bite-sized candy caramels (unwrapped)
3 cups pecan halves
2 tablespoons milk
1 cup semisweet chocolate morsels

Cookie base:

Cream shortening and sugars in a large bowl until fluffy. Add milk. Beat in eggs one at a time until fluffy. Add vanilla extract. Combine 4 and ½ cups flour, baking soda, cream of tartar and salt. Stir into creamed mixture. Chill one hour or overnight. Preheat oven

to 350 degrees. Roll out 1/3 of dough on floured board (if too sticky, add a bit more flour). Cut with 2 inch round cookie cutter about ¼ inch thickness. Place 2 inches apart on ungreased baking sheet. Bake 5 to 6 minutes until edges are slightly brown. Remove to cooling rack.

Topping:
Combine caramels and milk in microwave safe bowl. Heat in a microwave oven at 50% power for 1 minute. Stir. Repeat until mixture is smooth. Drop one teaspoonful of caramel topping in the center of each round cookie. Place 3 pecan halves, equi-distance on top, of each cookie. Allow to set up. Then place chocolate morsels into microwave safe bowl. Heat in a microwave oven 50% power for 1 minute. Stir. Repeat until mixture is smooth. Add a small dollop of chocolate to the top of caramel in the center of the cookie. No need to cover pecans. Cool cookies completely before storing.

Carmen Grimm

Chocolate Dipped Butter Cookie

1 cup butter, softened
½ cup confectioners' sugar
1 teaspoon vanilla extract
2 cups all purpose flour

1 cup chocolate morsels
3 tablespoons butter
Dry roasted peanuts, chopped

Beat butter and confectioners' sugar till fluffy. Blend in 1 cup flour. Add 1 teaspoon vanilla extract and remaining flour. Mix until well blended. Roll a large spoonful into a log and cut into 2-inch lengths. Place on a cookie sheet or pan lined with wax paper. Continue until all dough is used. Freeze the butter cookie logs.

Remove from freezer and place on a cookie sheet lined with parchment paper.

Bake frozen at 350 degrees for 12 to 14 minutes. (Make sure they are frozen or the butter will melt out of them before they are baked.) Cool on a wire rack.

Mix 1 cup chocolate morsels and 3 tablespoons butter. Melt in microwave oven and stir. Put chopped dry roasted peanuts in a separate bowl.

When cookies are completely cooled, dip them in melted chocolate and peanuts. Cool on wax paper.

Andrea Haldy

Sunday School Cookies
Gingerbread Boys & Girls

¾ cup granulated sugar
2/3 cup butter or margarine, softened
¼ cup orange juice
½ cup dark corn syrup
½ cup dark molasses
4 ½ cups all purpose flour
¾ cup whole wheat flour

2 teaspoons ground ginger
1 teaspoon baking soda
1 teaspoon salt
½ teaspoon ground cloves
½ teaspoon ground nutmeg
½ teaspoon allspice

Cream sugar and butter in a mixing bowl. Blend in orange juice, corn syrup and molasses. Combine dry ingredients and add to creamed mixture. Mix well. Chill 3 to 4 hours or overnight. Roll dough, a portion at a time, on a lightly floured surface to ¼-inch thickness. Using cookie cutters shaped like a boy and a girl or your own favorite cookie cutters, cut into desired shapes. Place 2 inches apart on greased cookie sheets. Bake at 350 degrees for 12 to 14 minutes. Cookies will be soft and chewy if baked 12 minutes and crunchy if baked longer.

Yield: 6 to 7 dozen

Elsie Sayers

Sugar Plums

1 cup butter
½ cup confectioners' sugar
½ teaspoon vanilla extract
2 cups sifted all purpose flour
½ teaspoon salt
1 cup oatmeal
2 dozen candied cherries

Beat butter to soften and then add sugar and vanilla. Sift flour and salt together and add to butter mixture. Stir in oatmeal. Shape into balls about 1- inch in diameter. Make a thumbprint in the middle of the ball and place a candied cherry into the hole left by the thumb. "Build" up the dough around the cherry as needed to keep the cherry in place but do not cover the cherry completely. Bake at 325 degrees for 30 minutes. After baking leave the cookies on the baking sheet for at least one minute and then roll the cookies in confectioners' sugar.

Yield: 2 dozen

Elsie Sayers

Norwegian Pepper Cookies

1 cup granulated sugar
1 cup dark corn syrup
1 cup butter
1 tablespoon vinegar
2 eggs, slightly beaten
5 cups all purpose flour

1 ½ teaspoons ground black pepper
1 teaspoon ground ginger
1 teaspoon ground cloves
1 teaspoon ground cinnamon
1 teaspoon baking soda

Combine sugar, corn syrup, butter and vinegar in a small pan and bring almost to a boil. Cool to room temperature. Stir in eggs. Sift together remaining ingredients and stir into butter mixture; blend well. Chill overnight.

Preheat oven to 350 degrees. Divide chilled dough into several portions and roll out each on a floured board until very thin. Cut into small (3 inch or less) shapes with a cookie cutter and place on a greased cookie sheets. Bake at 350 degrees for 7 to 8 minutes.

Yield: 18 dozen

Southwest Butter Pecan Cookies

½ cup butter, softened
½ cup granulated sugar
1 cup brown sugar, firmly packed
1 egg
½ teaspoon salt

1 ½ teaspoons vanilla extract
1 ½ cups all purpose flour
1 to 2 teaspoons chili powder
  (depending on your taste)
1 cup pecans, finely chopped

Mexican chocolate icing:
1/3 cup dark or bittersweet chocolate
¼ teaspoon chili powder

½ teaspoon cinnamon

Cookies:

Preheat oven to 375 degrees. Beat butter and sugars until light and fluffy. Add egg, salt and vanilla; blend until incorporated. Stir in flour and chili powder, blend well. Add pecans. Mix to combine. Shape dough into 1 inch balls. Bake for 12 to 15 minutes or until light brown at the edges. Cool on pan for two minutes or until set, then remove and allow to cool completely.

Mexican chocolate icing:

Microwave chocolate 30 seconds, stir then continue at 10 to 20 second intervals until melted and stirred smooth. Add chili powder and cinnamon. Using teaspoon, drizzle chocolate over cookies. Store in an airtight container at room temperature, separating layers with parchment paper.   **Yield:** 4 to 5 dozen

Christmas Rainbows

8 ounces almond paste
1 cup butter, softened
1 cup granulated sugar
4 eggs, separated
2 cups all purpose flour
Red and green food coloring

¼ cup blackberry jelly
¼ cup apricot jam (strained)
1 cup semisweet chocolate morsels

Line 3 cookie sheets with parchment paper.
In a large mixing bowl, break up almond paste with fork. Add butter, sugar and egg yolks and cream until fluffy. Stir in flour. In a separate bowl beat egg whites till stiff peaks form. Fold whites into the batter. Divide dough into 3 equal portions. Color one portion with red food coloring, one portion with green and leave one uncolored. Spread each portion onto a baking sheet and bake at 350 degrees for 10 to 12 minutes until edges start to brown. Invert onto wire racks and remove parchment paper. Cool.
Place green layer on plastic wrap and spread with blackberry jelly, then place white layer and spread the apricot jam and finish by placing the red layer on top. Let cool completely.
Melt chocolate and spread on top. Allow to harden. Trim edges.
Cut into ½-inch wide strips and then cut each strip into 4 to 5 pieces.

Yield: 8 dozen

Susan Shoup

Chocolate Covered Cherry Cookies

Chocolate Covered Cherry Cookies:

½ cup butter or margarine
1 cup granulated sugar
1 egg
1 ½ teaspoon vanilla extract
1 ½ cups all purpose flour

½ cup baking cocoa powder
¼ teaspoon salt
¼ teaspoon baking powder
¼ teaspoon baking soda
48 maraschino cherries, blotted dry

Frosting:

1 cup semi-sweet chocolate morsels
1 to 3 teaspoons maraschino cherry juice
½ cup sweetened condensed milk

In a mixing bowl, cream together butter and sugar until fluffy; beat in egg and vanilla.
Combine the dry ingredients; gradually add to creamed mixture (batter will be very firm).
Shape into 48 balls about 1 inch round and place on ungreased cookie sheets.
Push one cherry halfway into each ball.

Chocolate Covered Cherry Cookies (continued from pg 38)

Frosting:
Melt chocolate morsels and milk in a small saucepan over low heat, stirring constantly. Remove from heat; add cherry juice and stir until smooth. Spoon 1 teaspoon of frosting over each cherry. The frosting will spread over cookies during baking.
Bake at 350 degrees for 10 to 12 minutes. Cool on wire rack.

Yield: 4 dozen

Elsie Sayers and Marie Kinyon

Christmas Balls

1 cup butter
1 cup margarine
4 teaspoons vanilla
2/3 cup granulated sugar

4 teaspoons water
4 cups all purpose flour
2 cups finely ground nuts
Colored sugar

Cream butter, margarine and sugar until fluffy. Blend in vanilla extract and water. Add flour and blend well. Add nuts and blend well. Form into 1-inch balls and roll in colored sugar. Place on cookie sheets.
Bake at 325 degrees for 20 minutes.

Betty Graesser

Buttery Sugar Cut-out Cookies

1 ½ cups butter, softened
2 large eggs
1 ½ cups granulated sugar
2 teaspoons vanilla extract

½ teaspoon salt
½ teaspoon baking soda
4 cups all purpose flour

In a large mixing bowl, cream butter and sugar until fluffy. Beat in eggs, vanilla and baking soda. Gradually blend in flour; beat until creamy. Refrigerate dough until hard at least 2 hours.

Line cookie sheets with parchment paper. Preheat oven to 375 degrees. Choose your favorite cookie cutters. Working with only part of the dough at one time while keeping the rest chilled, flour board well and roll out. **Hint:** use a piece of floured parchment between your rolling pin and the dough itself so that the dough won't stick to the rolling pin.

Roll out to desired thickness – these cookies don't rise a lot but they do rise a bit, so roll out to less than ½ inch. If the dough is too sticky, put it back in the refrigerator. Chilled dough is much less difficult to work with. Cut out cookies and place on ungreased parchment paper.

Bake at 375 degrees 8 to 9 minutes (depending on how thick the cookie is). When edges are just lightly brown, remove. Cool completely. Frost and decorate.

Yield: 3 to 4 dozen

Emilie Hoppe

Coconut Oatmeal Cookies

¾ cup shortening, butter or margarine
2 cups brown sugar, firmly packed
2 eggs, well beaten
1 cup flaked coconut
1 teaspoon baking soda in 2 tablespoons hot water
1 teaspoon baking powder
2 cups all purpose flour
3 cups oatmeal
Colored sugar for decorating

Cream shortening, butter or margarine and sugar until fluffy. Add in remaining ingredients in order given, mixing after each one. Mix well. Roll into balls the size of a walnut. Dip in white or colored sugar. Flatten slightly.
Bake at 350 degrees for approximately 13 minutes or until edges or lightly browned.

Marzipan

2 cups brown sugar, firmly packed
2 cups granulated sugar
8 eggs
2 tablespoons butter
2 teaspoons baking soda

2 teaspoons baking powder
1 teaspoon nutmeg
1 teaspoon cinnamon
9 to 10 cups all purpose flour

Beat eggs until lemon colored. Blend all ingredients - except flour - with eggs in a very large bowl. Add flour one cup at a time while stirring. The amount of flour will depend on how wet the dough feels; the dough needs to be able to be rolled out, but can be sticky as flour will be worked in while rolling the dough.

Roll out dough on a well-floured surface. Work flour into the dough if dough is sticking to the rolling pin. Roll to about ½-inch thick. Cut into desired shapes with cookie cutters and place on a large cutting board or cookie sheets (can place close together). Prick each cookie with a pin 5 to 6 times. If not using an old Amana tin cookie cutter (which creates indented patterns) use a thimble to make indented patterns in the cookie.

Cover with a cotton dish towel. Place in a cool spot. Let cookies rest for 12 to 24 hours. Resting the cookies for at least 12 hours is a must so that the dough can aerate and mellow. Cookie dough will rise just a bit and form a slight crust on the top.

Place on greased cookie sheets bake at 325 degrees for 8 minutes.

Yield: 8 to 10 dozen

Marlene Trumpold

Amana Merba

Dough:
1 cup butter, softened (2 sticks)
4 eggs, hard boiled
Lemon zest
½ cup granulated sugar
vanilla extract
2 cups all purpose flour

Topping:
2 egg whites, raw
1 cup almonds, finely chopped
2 tablespoons decorative sugar

Hard boil 4 eggs. Use only the yolks (enjoy the whites on your salad). Prepare the dough by creaming the butter, hard boiled yolks, sugar, lemon zest and a dash vanilla extract together. Once well mixed, add flour.
Separate 2 eggs and place egg whites into a small bowl and set aside. Use a food processor or blender to finely chop the almonds (almost to a powder). In a small bowl combine chopped almonds with decorative sugar (sometimes called sparkling sugar). Roll out dough to 1/8 inch thick on a well-floured surface. Use a 2-inch diameter round cookie cutter (a fluted edge adds a nice touch) to cut out cookies. Dip the top of the cookie in egg whites and then in the nut /sugar mixture. Place on an ungreased cookie sheet and bake at 325 degrees for 6 to 8 minutes.

Yield: 6 dozen

Marlene Trumpold

Mistletoe Mint Cookies

3/4 cup (1/2 margarine, 1/2 butter)
2 cups chocolate morsels
1½ cups brown sugar, firmly packed
2 tablespoons water
2 eggs

2½ cups all purpose flour
1¼ teaspoons baking soda
½ teaspoon salt
2 boxes (6 ounces each) Andes Mint
   candies, each candy cut into fourths

Melt butter and chocolate morsels stirring until partially melted. Remove from heat and stir until chips are completely melted. Combine melted chocolate, brown sugar and water in a large bowl. Cool slightly. Beat in eggs one at a time at high speed. Reduce to low speed and add dry ingredients. Stir until blended. Chill dough.

Preheat oven to 350 degrees. Roll dough into very small balls (less than 1 teaspoon per ball) and place 2 inches apart on an ungreased cookie sheet. Bake for 8 to10 minutes, until the cookies have flattened and started to crack. Remove from the oven and place a piece of the Andes mint candy on each cookie, while cookie is still hot. Use the back of a spoon to swirl the melted Andes Mint candy across the top of the cookie. Remove to cooling rack to cool completely.

Yield: 8 dozen

Marlene Trumpold

Wiesbader Brot

1 cup butter, melted
2 cups granulated sugar
1 teaspoon cinnamon
4 eggs
2 teaspoons baking powder
6 cups all purpose flour
Colored sugar (for decorating)

Separate two of the four eggs.
Reserve the 2 egg yolks, beat and set aside for the glaze.
Mix the remaining ingredients - including 2 whole eggs and the 2 egg whites - together in a very large bowl. Roll out dough to ¼-inch thick on a well-floured surface. Use cookie cutters to cut into desired shapes. Place on greased cookie sheets and use a pastry brush to glaze with the beaten egg yolks. Sprinkle with colored sugar. Bake in a preheated 350 degrees for 8-10 minutes.

Yield: 8 to 9 dozen

Marlene Trumpold

Cottage Cheese Cookies

Cookies:
2 cups all-purpose flour—sift after it is measured
1 cup (2 sticks) cold butter—slice into pats
1 cup plus 2 tablespoons cottage cheese, cream style, small curd
Raspberry preserves—approximately 9 ounces

Glaze:
1 cup confectioners' sugar
Milk—just enough to make a drizzle icing.
2 teaspoons almond extract
Decorative colored sugar

Place flour in medium bowl. Cut in butter as you do for a pie crust. Add cottage cheese and mix until a sticky ball forms. Wrap in plastic wrap and chill in refrigerator for at least 2 to 3 hours or overnight. Place ½ of chilled dough on a lightly-floured board. Use as little flour as possible to roll out. Return other half to refrigerator. Lightly flour the top. With rolling pin, roll dough into a rectangle about 22 inches by 9 inches, 1/8-inch thick. Cut with a 3-inch round cookie cutter. Take "scraps" of raw dough and roll and cut until all dough is used. While cut out dough is on the floured surface, place a ¼ teaspoon of preserves in center of each circle.

Take your finger tip and dip into water and wet the edge of dough to moisten.
Flip one side of dough onto the other to form a little turnover. With floured fork, pinch the edge to seal. Gently place on a lightly greased, heavy cookie sheet. Bake at 395 to 400 degrees for approximately 10 to 12 minutes. Cool on wire rack, then drizzle with glaze. Repeat with second half of chilled dough.
Sprinkle with red and green sugar while frosting is wet.

Note: Must use a heavy cookie sheet to avoid burning the bottoms of the cookies. Top of cookies do not brown all over. Bottom of cookie should be a light, golden brown. The ¼ teaspoon of preserves is enough—do not add extra as it will force its way out of dough and preserves will burn.

Yield: 4 dozen

Vicki R. Conley

Matcha Tea Balls

½ cup butter, softened
1 tablespoon matcha (green tea powder)
2 teaspoons ground ginger
1 tablespoon vanilla extract
1 teaspoon lemon zest
1 cup brown sugar, firmly packed

1 teaspoon baking powder
½ teaspoon baking soda
¼ teaspoon salt
2 eggs
2 1/2 cups all purpose flour

1 cup white chocolate morsels for drizzling

Beat butter, matcha, ginger, vanilla extract and lemon zest in a large bowl on medium speed until combined. Add brown sugar, baking powder, baking soda, and salt. Beat until light and fluffy. Beat in eggs, then flour. Cover and chill dough 1 hour or until easy to handle.

Preheat oven to 350 degrees. Shape dough into 1-inch balls. Place 2 inches apart on an ungreased cookie sheet. Bake 10 to 12 minutes or until light brown. Cool on a cookie sheet for 2 minutes and then move to wire rack to finish cooling.

Melt white chocolate morsels and drizzle over cookies

Betsy Momany

Spritz

1 ½ cups butter, softened
1 cup granulated sugar
1 teaspoon baking powder
1 egg
1 teaspoon vanilla extract
3 ½ cups all purpose flour

Food coloring paste (if desired; green for trees, red for poinsettias, etc.)

Preheat oven to 375 degrees. Beat butter in a large mixing bowl with an electric mixer on medium speed for 30 seconds. Add sugar and baking powder and beat well.
Add egg, vanilla, and food coloring (if using). Beat until well combined. Beat in as much flour as you can. Stir in any remaining flour. Do not chill dough.
Pack dough into a cookie press. Force dough through press onto ungreased cookie sheets. Bake at 375 degrees for 8 to 10 minutes or until edges of cookies are firm but not brown. Remove cookies and cool on wire racks.

Yield: 7 dozen

Betsy Momany

Santa's Shortbread Buttons

¾ cup butter, softened
¼ cup granulated sugar
2 cups all purpose flour
½ teaspoon flavoring (either vanilla or almond extract)
1/4 to 1/2 teaspoon food coloring paste

Heat oven to 350 degrees. Beat butter and sugar in large bowl with electric mixer
on medium speed till fluffy. Stir in flour and flavoring. If dough is crumby, mix in an
additional 1 to 2 tablespoons softened butter. Choose a color and beat in food coloring
till well mixed.

Roll dough ¼-inch thick on a lightly floured surface. Cut with a 1 ½ - inch diameter
round cookie cutter. Use a slightly smaller round cookie cutter or glass to make an
indent inside the cut-out cookie (this is the edge of your button) Make four "buttonholes"
in the middle of the cut-out using a toothpick or straw. Bake 10-12 minutes. Remove
from cookie sheet to cool on wire rack.

Yield: 3 dozen

Betsy Momany

Snowcapped Gingersnaps

1 cup brown sugar, firmly packed
¾ cup butter
¼ cup unsulphured molasses
1 egg
2 ¼ cups all purpose flour
2 teaspoons baking soda
Topping:
18 1 ounce squares white baking chocolate, broken into pieces
1 tablespoon shortening

1 teaspoon ground cinnamon
1 teaspoon ginger
½ teaspoon ground cloves
¼ teaspoon salt
white granulated sugar (for rolling)

Beat brown sugar, butter, molasses, and egg in a large bowl with electric mixer on medium speed. Stir in flour, baking soda, cinnamon, ginger, ground cloves, and salt. Cover and refrigerate at least 1 hour.

Preheat oven to 375 degrees. Lightly grease cookie sheet. Shape dough by rounded teaspoonfuls into balls. Roll in white sugar and place balls about 3 inches apart on cookie sheet. Bake 9-12 minutes or just until set. Remove from cookie sheet to wire rack to cool.

Melt broken white chocolate baking squares and shortening in microwave for 1 to 2 minutes, stirring every 15 seconds. Dip half of cookie in chocolate and then place on parchment paper to dry.

Yield: 4 dozen

Betsy Momany

Cherry Jewels

1 cup butter, softened
½ cup granulated sugar
1/3 cup light corn syrup
2 egg yolks
½ teaspoon vanilla extract
2 ½ cups all purpose flour
1 jar maraschino cherries (drained & halved; pat dry with a paper towel)

In large bowl, cream butter and sugar until fluffy. Beat in corn syrup, egg yolks and vanilla. Gradually add flour and mix well. Cover and refrigerate several hours.
Roll into 1-inch balls. Place on ungreased baking sheets. Using end of wooden spoon handle, make an indentation in center of each ball. Press cherry half in center.
Bake at 325 degrees for 14 to 16 minutes.

Yield: 5 dozen

Mildred Setzer

The Real Deal Monster Cookie

6 eggs
2 ¼ cups brown sugar, firmly packed
2 cups granulated sugar
2 ½ cups chunky peanut butter
1 cup butter, softened
2 teaspoons vanilla extract

2 teaspoons light corn syrup
4 teaspoons baking soda
9 cups quick cooking oatmeal
1 cup milk chocolate, plain, M&Ms
1 cup semi-sweet chocolate morsels
½ cup flaked sweetened coconut

In large bowl, combine eggs, sugars, peanut butter, butter or margarine, vanilla, corn syrup and baking soda. Mix well. Add oats, M&Ms, chocolate chips and flaked coconut. Blend thoroughly. Drop dough from ice cream scoop or ¼ cup measuring cup onto cookie sheets. Flatten slightly with bottom of glass dipped in sugar.
Bake at 350 degrees for 12 to 15 minutes until edges begin to brown.
Cool slightly before removing from pan.

Yield: 4 – 5 dozen

Toffee Almond Sandies

1 ¾ cup all purpose flour
½ cup whole wheat flour
½ teaspoon baking soda
½ teaspoon cream of tartar
½ teaspoon salt
½ cup butter, softened (1 stick)
½ cup granulated sugar

½ cup confectioners' sugar
½ cup vegetable oil
1 egg
½ teaspoon almond extract
1 cup chopped almonds
½ cup toffee bits (3 ounces)

Topping:
granulated sugar

Preheat oven to 350 degrees. Line 2 baking sheets with parchment paper. Combine flours, baking soda, cream of tartar and salt in medium bowl; mix well. In another bowl, cream butter, sugar, confectioners' sugar until well combined, 1 to 2 minutes. Scrape down sides of bowl, then add oil, egg and almond extract; mix well. Add dry ingredients and mix slowly to combine. Stir in almonds and toffee bits. Shape into 1-inch balls; roll in sugar. Place about 2 inches apart on lined baking sheets and flatten with a fork. Bake for 14 to 17 minutes or until lightly browned, rotating sheets a halfway through baking. Let cool on baking sheets for a few minutes then transfer to wire rack to cool completely.

Yield: 4 to 5 dozen

Chocolate Mint Whoopie Pies

½ cup granulated sugar
3 tablespoons canola oil
1 egg
1 cup all purpose flour
¼ cup baking soda
¼ teaspoon salt

4 tablespoons fat-free milk, divided
2 tablespoons butter, softened
1 1/3 cups confectioners' sugar
1/8 teaspoon pure peppermint extract
4 drops green food coloring, optional

In bowl, beat sugar and oil until crumbly. Add egg; beat for 1 minute. Combine flour, cocoa, baking soda and salt. Gradually beat into sugar mixture. Add 2 tablespoons milk; mix well. With lightly floured hands, roll dough into 36 balls.

Place 2 inches apart on baking sheets coated with nonstick cooking spray. Flatten slightly with a glass coated with cooking spray. Bake at 425 degrees for 5 to 6 minutes or until edges are set and tops are cracked. Cool for 2 minutes before removing to wire racks to cool.

In mixing bowl, combine butter and confectioners' sugar until fluffy. Beat in peppermint extract, food coloring and remaining milk. Spread on half of the cookies; top with remaining cookies.

Yield: 1 ½ dozen

Susan Shoup

Lemon Tea Cookies

¾ cup butter, softened
½ cup granulated sugar
1 egg yolk
½ teaspoon vanilla extract
2 cups all purpose flour
¼ cup finely chopped walnuts

Filling:
3 tablespoons butter, softened
4 ½ teaspoons lemon juice
¾ teaspoon grated orange peel
1 ½ cups confectioners' sugar
2 drops yellow food coloring, optional

In a large mixing bowl, cream butter and sugar until light and fluffy. Beat in the egg yolk and vanilla. Gradually add flour. Shape into two 14-inch rolls – each roll about 1 and 1/8 inch thick. Then pat and shape each log into a long block with flat sides. Wrap each long block in plastic wrap. Refrigerate overnight.

Unwrap and cut into ¼-inch slices. Place 2 inches apart on ungreased baking sheets. Sprinkle half of the cookies with nuts, gently pressing the nuts into the dough. Bake at 400 degrees for 8 to 10 minutes or until golden brown around the edges. Remove to wire racks to cool.

Filling: in a small mixing bowl, cream butter, lemon juice and orange peel. Gradually add confectioners' sugar. Tint yellow if desired. Spread about 1 teaspoonful on top of plain cookie; place nut topped cookie on filling. Thus you create little square sandwiches with the finely chopped nuts on top.

Yield: 4 ½ dozen

Susan Shoup

Potato Chip Cookies

2 cups butter, softened (no substitutes)
1 cup granulated sugar
4 cups all purpose flour
2 teaspoons vanilla extract
1 cup crushed potato chips
1 cup chopped pecans

Cream butter and sugar in a large mixing bowl. Gradually add flour, beating until combined. Beat in vanilla. Stir in potato chips and pecans. Cover and refrigerate for 1 hour.
Drop dough by tablespoonfuls onto ungreased baking sheet, 2 inches apart. Bake at 350 degrees for 12 to 15 minutes or until golden brown. Remove to wire racks to cool.

Yield: 5 dozen

Florence Schuerer

Reese's Peanut Butter Cup Cookies

1 3/4 cups all purpose flour
1 teaspoon baking soda
1/2 teaspoon salt
1/2 cup butter, softened
1/2 cup creamy peanut butter
1/2 cup granulated sugar

1/2 cup brown sugar, firmly packed
1 egg
2 tablespoon milk
1 teaspoon vanilla extract
1 12 ounce bag of miniature Reese's
Peanut Butter Cups, remove all wrappers

You'll need a mini muffin tin and mini paper liners.

Sift flour, baking soda and salt. Cream butter and peanut butter; gradually add sugars and cream well. Add egg, milk and vanilla. Beat well. Gradually blend in dry ingredients; mix thoroughly. Refrigerate for an hour or overnight. Place mini cupcake paper liners in mini muffin tin. Roll dough into 1-inch sized ball and place in each liner.
Bake at 350 degrees for 8 to 10 minutes. Take pan out and immediately, push one peanut butter cup into each cookie and return the pan to the oven for 2 to 5 minutes. Remove and cool completely before removing from the pan.

Yield: 2 dozen.

Susan Hollrah

Chocolate Oatmeal Cookies

1/2 cup butter, softened
1 cup granulated sugar
1 egg, slightly beaten
2 1 ounce squares semi-sweet chocolate, melted
1 teaspoon vanilla extract
1/2 teaspoon salt
1 teaspoon baking powder
1 cup all purpose flour
1 1/2 cups oatmeal
1 10 ounce package chocolate mini morsels

Mix butter and sugar, add the egg, melted chocolate and vanilla. Sift flour, baking powder and salt together and add to the creamed batter along with oatmeal and mini chocolate chips. Drop by teaspoonfuls onto a greased cookie sheet. Press flat with the flat-side of a knife dipped in cold water or a glass.
Bake at 350 degrees for 10 to 12 minutes.

Yield: 2 dozen

Susan Hollrah

Snowballs
(No Bake Cookies)

1 cup butter, softened
1/2 cup creamy peanut butter, smooth
3 cups confectioners' sugar
1 cup mini chocolate morsels
2 cups oatmeal
1/2 teaspoon vanilla extract

Mix all ingredients together. Roll into small "snowballs" and roll in confectioners' sugar. Chill. Store in an air-tight container, covered, in the refrigerator.

Note: this is the perfect recipe to make with young children as it's a no-fail, no-bake cookie.

Susan Hollrah

Sprinkle Cookies

1 cup unsalted butter, softened
1 cup granulated sugar
1 large egg
1 teaspoon almond extract
2 ½ cups all purpose flour
1 teaspoon kosher salt
½ cup Christmas colored sprinkles

Preheat oven to 350 degrees. Line baking sheets with parchment paper.
In a large bowl, beat butter and sugar with mixer at medium speed until fluffy, about 3 to 4 minutes, stopping to scrape down sides of bowl. Add egg and almond extract.
In a medium bowl, whisk together flour and salt. Gradually add flour mixture to butter mixture, beating until just combined. Shape dough into 1-inch balls; roll in sprinkles.
Place at least 2 inches apart on prepared pans. Flatten slightly with the bottom of a glass. Freeze until firm, about 15 minutes.
Bake 12 to 15 minutes until edges are slightly browned. Let cool on pans 2 minutes. Remove from pans, and let cool completely on wire racks. Store in airtight containers up to 3 days.

Terry Roemig

Chocolate Peanut Butter Swirl Cookies

Peanut butter dough:
¾ cup peanut butter
½ cup butter, softened
½ cup granulated sugar
½ cup brown sugar, firmly packed
1 egg
1 1/4 cups all purpose flour
½ teaspoon baking powder
½ teaspoon baking soda
¼ teaspoon salt

Chocolate dough:
½ cup butter, softened
½ cup granulated sugar
½ cup brown sugar, firmly packed
1 egg
1 teaspoon vanilla extract
1 1/4 cups all purpose flour
¼ cup cocoa
½ teaspoon baking powder
½ teaspoon baking soda
¼ teaspoon salt

For peanut butter dough: in a large bowl cream peanut butter, butter and sugars until light and fluffy; about 4 minutes. Beat in egg. Combine flour, baking powder, baking soda and salt; gradually add to creamed mixture and mix well.

For chocolate dough: in a second large bowl cream butter and sugars until light and fluffy. Beat in egg and vanilla. Combine flour, cocoa, baking powder, baking soda and salt; gradually add to creamed mixture and mix well.

Chocolate Peanut Butter Swirl Cookies (continued from pg 64)

Divide each portion in half. Knead one peanut butter and one chocolate portion together 5-10 times or until dough just begins to swirl. Shape into a 10-inch log. Wrap in plastic. Repeat with remaining dough. Refrigerate 3 to 4 hours or until firm.
Preheat oven to 350 degrees. Unwrap and cut into ¼-inch thick slices. Place 2 inches apart on lightly greased baking sheets. Bake 6 to 8 minutes or until bottoms are lightly browned. Cool 2 minutes before removing from pan to wire racks.

Freeze option: Place wrapped dough logs in resealable plastic freezer bag; freeze. To use, unwrap frozen logs and slice to ¼-inch thickness. If necessary, let dough stand a few minutes at room temperature before cutting. Bake as directed.

Yield: 6 – 7 dozen

Raspberry Sandwich Spritz

1 cup butter, softened
¾ cup granulated sugar
1 egg
1 teaspoon vanilla extract
2 ¼ cups all purpose flour

½ teaspoon salt
¼ teaspoon baking powder
1 cup seedless raspberry jam
1 cup semi-sweet chocolate morsels
chocolate sprinkles

In large mixing bowl, cream butter and sugar. Beat in egg and vanilla.
Combine flour, salt and baking powder; gradually add to creamed mixture.
Using a cookie press fitted with ribbon disk, form dough into long strips on ungreased baking sheets. Cut each strip into 2-inch pieces (do not separate).
Bake at 375 degrees for 8 to 10 minutes or until edges are golden brown.
Cut again if necessary. Remove to wire racks to cool.
Spread the bottom half of the cookies with jam; top with cookie.
In microwave, melt chocolate morsels; stir until smooth. Place chocolate sprinkles in bowl. Dip each end of cookie in melted chocolate then in sprinkles. Place on waxed paper; let dry until firm.

Yield: about 4 ½ dozen cookies

Susan Shoup

Best Sugar Cookies

1 cup butter or margarine
1 cup sugar
2 eggs
2 tablespoons milk
2 teaspoons vanilla extract
3 ¾ cup all purpose flour
1 teaspoon baking soda
½ teaspoon cream of tartar

Cream butter and sugar. Add eggs, beaten with milk and vanilla. Mix well.
Add sifted dry ingredients. Refrigerate for 1 hour. Roll out on lightly floured surface.
Cut out cookies with floured cookie cutters. Place on greased cookie sheets.
Bake at 375 degrees for 8 to 10 minutes or until lightly brown.
May be decorated with frosting and colored sugar.

Dorothy Marz and Terry Roemig

Café Mocha Cookies

3/4 cup salted butter, softened
1 cup dark brown sugar
1/2 cup granulated sugar
1 large egg
1 teaspoon vanilla extract
3 tablespoons brewed dark roast coffee
2 cups all purpose flour

1/2 cup unsweetened dark cocoa
1 1/2 tablespoons finely ground coffee
1 1/2 teaspoons baking soda
1 teaspoon salt
3/4 cup semi-sweet chocolate morsels
3/4 cup Nestle espresso morsels

Preheat the oven to 350°F. Combine butter, sugars, egg, vanilla and coffee; beat on medium speed until creamy and smooth.

In a separate bowl, combine the flour, cocoa powder, ground coffee, baking soda and salt. Mix well. Gradually add to the butter mixture and beat until just combined. Stir in the chocolate chips and espresso morsels.

Roll tablespoon (or slightly larger) balls of batter and place on baking sheet, approx. 2 inches apart. Bake in the preheated oven for 9 to 11 minutes, or until the centers of the cookies are cooked through. Remove from the oven, transfer the cookies to a wire rack and let cool.

Erin Wilding

Holiday Wreaths

1/3 cup butter or margarine
1 (10 oz.) package large marshmallows (about 40)
1 teaspoon green food coloring liquid
6 cups cornflakes
Red cinnamon candies

Melt butter in large saucepan over low heat. Add marshmallows, stirring constantly, until marshmallows melt and mixture is syrupy. Remove from heat.
Stir in food coloring. Add cereal and stir until well coated.
Using a ¼ cup dry measuring cup, portion the warm cornflakes mixture.
With your fingers buttered quickly shape into individual wreaths.
Dot each with red cinnamon candies.

Yield: 16 wreaths

Carol S. Zuber

Lunch Box Jumble Cookies

1/2 cup vegetable shortening
2 cup granulated sugar
2 eggs
1/4 cup brewed coffee, cold
3 squares unsweetened baking chocolate, melted

3 1/2 cups all purpose flour
4 teaspoons baking powder
1/2 teaspoon salt
1 teaspoon cinnamon

Topping:
1 cup finely chopped nuts
2 tablespoons granulated sugar
1/2 teaspoon cinnamon

Cream shortening and sugar. Beat eggs and coffee together; add to creamed mixture.
Melt chocolate over hot water or in microwave oven; blend in.
Sift flour, baking powder, salt and cinnamon; blend in.
Roll dough out to 1/3-inch thickness on lightly floured board; cut with doughnut cutter.
Combine topping ingredients and sprinkle over cookies. press in.
Arrange on greased cookie sheet. Bake at 350 degrees for 12 minutes.

Yield: 4 dozen

Connie Baugh

Tante Dorothea's Chocolate Pinwheel Cookies

1 ½ cups butter
1 ½ cups sugar
3 egg yolks
2 tablespoons vanilla extract
3 tablespoons milk

4 ½ cups all purpose flour
1 ½ teaspoons baking powder
1 teaspoon salt
3 ounces unsweetened chocolate, melted
3 tablespoons milk

Thoroughly cream butter and sugar. Add egg yolks, vanilla extract and 3 tablespoons milk. Mix well. Sift flour, baking powder and salt. Stir into creamed mixture. Divide dough in half. To one part, add melted unsweetened chocolate and 3 tablespoons milk. Mix well. Refrigerate doughs. Between two pieces of plastic wrap, roll one third of chocolate dough into a rectangle. (The chocolate dough will be fairly stiff.) Do the same for one third of vanilla dough. Place the vanilla dough on the chocolate dough and roll up tightly. Repeat with remaining dough. Wrap dough rolls and chill or freeze. Heat oven to 375°. Cut rolls into 1/4-inch slices and place on greased baking sheets. Bake 8 to 10 minutes. Bottoms (only) shou'd be slightly browned. Immediately remove from baking sheet and cool.

Yield: 8 dozen

Mary Burgher

Bars

Butter Brickle Bars

Bars:
1 package yellow cake mix
1/3 cup margarine
1 egg

Topping:
1 egg
1 cup pecans, ground
1 8 ounce package Heath Bits' O Brickle
   (English toffee bits)
1 14 ounce can sweetened condensed milk

Mix bar ingredients like a pie crust and press into a jelly roll pan (15 x 10 inch).

Topping: Combine topping ingredients. Blend. Drop by teaspoonfuls onto the crust. As it is hard to spread, drop small amounts close together.

During baking topping spreads.

Bake 350 degrees for 30 minutes.

When cool, cut into small pieces.

Joanna Schanz

Favorite Oatmeal Bars

1 cup all purpose flour
1 cup quick cooking oatmeal
¾ cup brown sugar, firmly packed
½ cup butter, softened
1   14 ounce can sweetened condensed milk
1 cup chopped nuts
1 cup semi-sweet chocolate morsels

Preheat oven to 350 degrees (325 degrees for glass dish). Combine flour, oats, brown sugar and butter. Mix well. Reserving ½ cup, press remaining oat mixture in bottom of 13 x 9 inch baking pan.
Bake 10 minutes.
Pour sweetened condensed milk evenly over crust. Sprinkle with nuts and semi-sweet chocolate morsels. Top with remaining oat mixture; press down lightly.
Bake 25 to 30 minutes or until lightly browned. Cool.
Store covered at room temperature.

Cheesecake Bars

10 tablespoons butter (1 stick plus 2 tablespoons)
2/3 cup brown sugar, firmly packed
2 cups all purpose flour
1 cup chopped nuts
1 cup granulated sugar
2 8 ounce packages cream cheese
2 eggs
5 tablespoons milk
1 tablespoon lemon juice
½ teaspoon vanilla extract

Cream butter and brown sugar. Add flour and nuts and mix. Set aside 2 cups of the mixture for topping. Press remainder in bottom of 13 x 9 inch baking pan.
Bake at 350 degrees for 12 to 15 minutes.
Blend granulated sugar and cream cheese until smooth.
Add egg, milk, lemon juice and vanilla. Beat well. Spread over bottom crust. Sprinkle with reserved topping. Return to oven and bake for approximately 25 minutes. Cool then chill. Store in refrigerator. Cut into bite-sized servings.

Pecan Pie Bars

Crust:
2 cups all purpose flour
1 teaspoon baking powder
1/8 teaspoon salt
2/3 cup brown sugar, firmly packed
½ cup butter, softened

Filling:
4 eggs
½ cup brown sugar, firmly packed
1/3 cup all purpose flour
1 teaspoon salt
1 ½ cups dark corn syrup
2 teaspoons vanilla extract
¾ cup chopped pecans

Preheat oven to 325 degrees.

Sift flour, baking powder and salt. Stir in brown sugar. Cut in butter until well mixed.
Pat evenly into bottom of 13 x 9 inch pan. Bake for 12 minutes.
Beat eggs until well mixed. Add brown sugar, flour and salt; beat well. Add corn syrup
and vanilla. Mix well. Pour over the partly baked crust and sprinkle with pecans.
Return to oven and bake 40 to 50 minutes. Cut into squares while still warm.

Fudge Nut Bars

1 cup butter
2 cups brown sugar, firmly packed
2 eggs
2 teaspoons vanilla extract

2 ½ cups all purpose flour
1 teaspoon baking soda
1 teaspoon salt
3 cups quick cook oatmeal

Filling:
2 cups chocolate chips
1 14 ounce can sweetened condensed milk
2 tablespoons butter

½ teaspoon salt
2 teaspoons vanilla
optional: 1 cup chopped nuts

Cream butter and sugar. Mix in eggs and vanilla.
Sift together flour, soda and salt. Stir in oatmeal. Add dry ingredients to creamed mixture. Set aside while making filling.
For filling: Place chocolate chips, sweetened condensed milk, butter and salt together in double boiler on stove or in microwave oven. Melt and stir until mixture is smooth. Stir in vanilla and chopped nuts.
Spread about 2/3 oatmeal mixture on bottom of greased 15 ½ x 10 ½ x 1 inch pan. Cover with chocolate mixture. Dot remaining oatmeal mixture over filling and swirl. Bake at 350 degrees for 25 to 30 minutes.

Candies & Fudge

Apricot Almond Chewies

2 cups slivered almonds, toasted
4 cups finely chopped dried apricots
4 cups flaked sweetened coconut
1 14 ounce can sweetened condensed milk
3 tablespoons finely chopped pecans

Toast almonds: Place almonds in dry, nonstick skillet and cook over medium heat, stirring continually, until nuts are lightly browned.

Combine toasted almonds, chopped apricots, coconut and condensed milk.
Chill at least 2 hours.

Shape dough into 1-inch diameter balls. Place in smaller or miniature foil candy liners.
Top with a sprinkle of finely chopped pecans.

Yield: 6 dozen

Amana Church Youth Group

Amana Radarange Pecan Brittle

1 cup pecans, chopped
½ cup light corn syrup
1 cup granulated sugar
2 teaspoons butter
1 teaspoon vanilla extract
1 teaspoon baking soda

Combine pecans, corn syrup and sugar in a 1 ½ quart microwave safe bowl. In a microwave oven, heat on high for 4 minutes. Stir and heat for 4 more minutes. Add butter and vanilla. Heat in microwave for 2 more minutes. Add baking soda and stir gently. Spread on a greased jelly roll pan. Allow to cool completely. Break into pieces.

Dorothy Seifert

Caramel Chews

28 candy caramels, unwrapped
3 tablespoons margarine
2 tablespoons water
1 5 ounce can or canister crunchy chow mein noodles
1 cup peanuts
1 cup semi-sweet chocolate morsels
2 tablespoons water

Melt caramels, margarine and water in a saucepan over low heat and melt, stirring until smooth. Add noodles and peanuts. Toss until well coated.

Drop by rounded teaspoons onto lightly buttered cookie sheet.
Melt chocolate morsels with water in saucepan over low heat. Top chews with melted chocolate. Chill.

Yield: 2 ½ dozen

Amy Jacobson

Merry Bon Bons

½ cup butter
1 14 ounce can sweetened condensed milk
1 pound confectioners' sugar
1 teaspoon vanilla extract
1 21 ounce package flaked or shredded sweetened coconut
¾ cup mini dark or semisweet chocolate morsels
1 12 to 16 ounce package white chocolate bark or almond bark

In a double boiler, melt butter, then stir in condensed milk. Add confectioners' sugar and vanilla extract. Stir until smooth. Remove from heat. Fold in the coconut and at the end add chocolate morsels. (Mixture should be cool enough that morsels don't melt) Place in a bowl, cover tightly and refrigerate at least 8 hours.
Line two baking trays with parchment paper. Roll balls into the size of bonbons (smaller than ping pong balls). Place all on one sheet.
Break up the bark into smaller pieces. Melt in a double boiler or follow package instructions to melt carefully in microwave oven. Do not scorch. Use a skewer to pick up coconut balls and dip them into the melted bark. Place on a second wax paper lined baking sheet. Allow to set. Place the tray in refrigerator to totally chill. Once they have set up well, store bon bons in an airtight container in the refrigerator or in a cool spot away from any heat source.

Sharon's Peanut Clusters

6 squares chocolate almond bark
3 squares white almond bark
1 pound dry roasted peanuts, salted

In a colander, shake dust well from peanuts.
Melt chocolate and white almond bark in a 3 quart microwave safe casserole dish for 1 minute, stir, then continue for 30 second intervals until melted, stirring several times.
Mix peanuts with almond bark.
Set casserole dish on a warming tray. Using a teaspoon, spoon clusters on foil lined cookie sheet. Cool. Store after they are completely cooled and set.

Note: The warming tray keeps the bark soft no matter how long it takes you.

Yield: 3 dozen

Sharon Grimm

Aloha Brittle

2 teaspoons butter, divided
½ cup sweetened shredded coconut
1 cup granulated sugar
½ cup light corn syrup
1 jar (3 oz.) macadamia nuts

¼ cup chopped pecans
¼ cup chopped hazelnuts
1 teaspoon baking soda
1 teaspoon water
1 teaspoon vanilla extract

Butter a large baking sheet with 1 teaspoon butter. Sprinkle coconut in a 12-inch circle on the prepared pan. In a large heavy saucepan, combine the sugar and corn syrup. Cook over medium heat until a candy thermometer reads 240 degrees (soft-ball stage), stirring constantly. Stir in macadamia nuts, pecans, and remaining 1 teaspoon butter; cook and stir until mixture reads 300 degrees (hard-crack stage).

In a small bowl combine baking soda, water, and vanilla. Remove saucepan from the heat; stir in the baking soda mixture. Quickly pour over the coconut. Once the brittle is cool break into pieces.

Betsy Momany

Coconut Snowballs

¼ cup butter, melted
2 cups confectioners' sugar
2 cups shredded coconut
¼ cup evaporated milk
1 teaspoon vanilla extract

1 to 2 containers sanding sugar (any color)

Mix ingredients together – except sanding sugar. Chill mixture for 2 or more hours. Roll into ½-inch diameter balls. Roll each in sanding sugar.

Betsy Momany

Buckeyes

½ cup creamy peanut butter
¼ cup butter
½ teaspoon vanilla extract
1 1/2 cups confectioners' sugar
2 cups crispy rice cereal
1 package (12 ounce) semi-sweet chocolate morsels
1 tablespoon paraffin wax, food grade for dipping

Mix peanut butter, butter, and vanilla extract together in a medium bowl. Stir in confectioners' sugar, ½ cup at a time. Then fold in the rice cereal, using hands if necessary. Roll balls into small 1-inch diameter balls. Place balls on a cookie sheet and freeze for one hour.

Melt the semi-sweet chocolate morsels and paraffin (or use *Wilton EZ Thin* dipping aid) in a saucepan over low heat. Dip the frozen peanut butter balls into the melted chocolate. Place on a cookie sheet and let cool.

Betsy Momany

Divinity

2 1/2 cups white granulated sugar
½ cup light corn syrup
½ teaspoon salt
½ cup water
2 egg whites
1 teaspoon vanilla extract

Combine sugar, corn syrup, ½ teaspoon salt and ½ cup water in a 2-quart saucepan. Cook to hard ball stage (260 degrees) stirring only until sugar dissolves. Meanwhile, beat egg whites to stiff peaks. Gradually pour syrup over egg whites, beating at high speed on electric mixer. Add vanilla and beat for 4 to 5 minutes until candy holds its shape. Quickly drop from a teaspoon onto waxed paper.

Yield: makes 3 dozen

Betsy Momany

Caramels

1 cup butter
2 1/4 cups brown sugar
Dash salt
1 cup light corn syrup
1 14 ounce can sweetened condensed milk
1 teaspoon vanilla extract

Butter a 9 x 9 inch pan. Melt butter in a heavy 3-quart saucepan. Add sugar and salt; stir thoroughly. Stir in corn syrup and mix well. Gradually add sweetened condensed milk while stirring constantly. Cook and stir over medium heat to firm ball stage (245 degrees), about 12-15 minutes. Stir in vanilla and pour into pan.
Cool and cut into bite-sized squares.

Betsy Momany

Andes Mint Fudge

1 12 ounce can evaporated milk
4 cups granulated sugar
1 teaspoon cream of tartar
1 pound (4 sticks) butter
1 tablespoon vanilla
3 12 ounce bags semi-sweet chocolate morsels
2 10 ounce bags *Andes Crème de Menthe* baking chips

Place evaporated milk and sugar in a heavy saucepan. Bring to a rolling boil at medium heat. Once at a rolling boil, reduce heat and continue at a low boil for 6 full minutes, stirring constantly. After 6 full minutes, add cream of tartar and boil for one more minute, stirring constantly. Remove from heat. Add butter and chips / morsels, beating with hand-held mixer until melted. Add vanilla extract and beat for 3 to 4 minutes until no longer shiny, but has a smooth glossy look. Pour into 18 x 24 x 1 inch greased jelly roll pan. Refrigerate to cool until firm. Cut into bite-sized pieces.

Note: Fudge will be very firm when chilled but will soften at room temperature

Ric Gerard

Cranberry Pecan Coconut Fudge

1 12 ounce can evaporated milk
4 cups granulated sugar
1 teaspoon cream of tartar
2 cups chopped dried cranberries
1 1/2 cups chopped pecans

1 cup flaked coconut
1 pound (4 sticks) butter
5 10 ounce bags white vanilla morsels
1 tablespoon vanilla extract

Place evaporated milk and sugar in a heavy saucepan. Bring to a rolling boil on medium heat. Add chopped dried cranberries and bring back to rolling boil. Once returned to boil, reduce heat and continue under low boil for 6 full minutes, stirring constantly. After 6 full minutes, add cream of tartar and boil for 1 more minute, stirring constantly. Remove from heat. Add butter and vanilla morsels, beating with hand- held mixer until melted. Add vanilla, pecans, and coconut. Beat for 3 to 4 minutes until no longer shiny but has a smooth glossy look. Pour into 18 x 24 X 1 inch greased pan. Refrigerate to cool until firm. Cut into bite-sized pieces.

Note: Fudge will be very firm when chilled but will soften at room temperature.

Ric Gerard

Key Lime Fudge

3 tablespoons zest of fresh limes
1 12 ounce can evaporated milk
4 cups granulated sugar
3 ounce key lime juice
  (a bottled juice available at most grocers).

1 pound (4 sticks) butter
1 tablespoon vanilla extract
5 10 oz. bags of white chocolate morsels
1 teaspoon cream of tartar
green food coloring

Zest fresh limes and set aside. Place evaporated milk and sugar in a heavy saucepan. Bring to a rolling boil on medium heat. Add lime juice and lime zest. Reduce heat and continue at a low boil for 6 full minutes, stirring constantly. Add cream of tartar and boil for 1 more minute, stirring constantly. Remove from heat. Add butter and morsels, beating with hand-held mixer until melted. Add vanilla and a few drops of green food coloring. Beat for 3 to 4 minutes until no longer shiny, but has a smooth glossy look. Pour into 18 x 24 X 1 inch greased pan. Refrigerate to cool until firm. Cut into bite-sized pieces.

Note: Fudge will be very firm when chilled but will soften at room temperature.

Ric Gerard

Peanut Clusters

1 20 ounce package vanilla almond bark
2 cups chocolate morsels
1 cup chunky peanut butter
2 cups Spanish salted peanuts

Melt almond bark and chocolate chips in microwave. Stir in peanut butter and then peanuts. Drop with a teaspoon into the miniature sized paper or foil candy or cupcake liners. Store in airtight container, chilled.

Yield: 7 dozen

Mildred Setzer

Candy Cane Fudge

2 10 ounce packages vanilla or white chocolate baking morsels
1 14 ounce can sweetened condensed milk
½ teaspoon peppermint extract
1 dash red or green food coloring, optional
1 ½ cups crushed candy canes

Line 8-inch square baking pan with aluminum foil or parchment paper. Grease.
Combine baking chips and sweetened condensed milk and melt in double boiler or in a microwave oven while stirring frequently
Remove from heat and continue to stir until smooth. When morsels are completely melted, stir in peppermint extract, crushed candy canes and food coloring (if desired). Spread evenly in prepared pan. Chill for 2 hours. Cut into squares.

Yield: 2 ¼ pounds

Classic Peanut Brittle

1 cup corn syrup
1 cup granulated sugar
1 tablespoon butter

¼ teaspoon salt
2 cups raw peanuts
2 teaspoons baking soda

Tips: Buy good quality, shelled raw peanuts. Open a new package of baking soda as the baking soda must be fresh. Invest in a candy thermometer and use it.
Lightly grease a cookie sheet. A jelly roll pan works best when making one batch.
In a 4-quart saucepan, combine corn syrup, sugar, butter and salt. Place on medium heat – and while stirring constantly – cook till sugar dissolves. AFTER sugar is fully dissolved, stir in peanuts (if the sugar is not quite dissolved the peanuts will scorch). Stir constantly. Continue cooking until mixture reaches 290 degrees on the candy thermometer.
Remove from heat. Stir in baking soda. Pour candy on the prepared cookie sheet. Don't spread too thin. Desired thickness is about ¼ inch.   Allow to cool. Break into pieces.

Tyler Schumacher and Mary Anne Stumpff

Cinnamon Sugar Pretzels

1 16 ounce package round pretzels
2/3 cup vegetable oil
½ cup granulated sugar
2 1/2 teaspoons cinnamon

Stir together, oil, sugar and cinnamon. In a microwave safe bowl stir together pretzels and oil, sugar and cinnamon mixture. Heat in microwave oven for 3 minutes stopping each minute to stir. Pour onto a cookie sheet to allow to cool. Store in plastic bag or airtight container. To give as gifts, place in small plastic or paper bags tied with holiday ribbon.

Connie Baugh

English Toffee

1 pound pecan halves
1 pound (4 sticks) butter
2 cups granulated sugar
2 12 ounce packages semi-sweet chocolate morsels.

Tip: Use only the highest quality butter as it will contain less water.
Use a candy thermometer.

Spray a jelly roll pan with cooking spray. Arrange pecan halves evenly in the pan. Set aside. In a heavy skillet combine butter and sugar and place on medium heat; while stirring, bring to a boil. Do not cover, but continue cooking 6 to 10 minutes, stirring occasionally, till mixture reaches 290 to 300 degrees. Pour over pecans. Sprinkle 1 package chocolate morsels evenly over the top of the toffee.
Allow to toffee to set. After it has set up and chocolate is dry, turn toffee over and sprinkle the second package of morsels over the pecans. The heat will melt the morsels. When cool break into pieces.

Yield: 4 pounds

Lucille Krauss

Salted Nut Roll Bars

1 16 ounce jar dry roasted peanuts
1 14 ounce can sweetened condensed milk
6 ounces peanut butter morsels
6 ounces butterscotch morsels
1 package mini marshmallows

Line a 9 x 13 inch pan with foil, leaving extra foil over edge to lift out bars.
Spray foil with cooking oil.
Spread 1/2 of the nuts on the foil.
Stirring often, melt the peanut butter morsels and the butterscotch morsels together
with the sweetened condensed milk until melted and smooth. Add marshmallows
and stir until smooth. (You may need to heat or warm in the microwave again.) Pour
mixture over the nuts. Sprinkle remaining half of the nuts on top. Slightly press nuts into
marshmallow mixture. Cool.
Lift bars out of pan with foil. Cut into small bars.

Connie Baugh

New Year's Pretzel

2 cups (2 %) milk, warmed
½ cup sugar
2 teaspoons salt
2 eggs, beaten

2 envelopes rapid rise yeast
½ cup vegetable oil
7 to 7 ½ cups all purpose flour

In a very large bowl, stir together (with a wooden spoon) warmed milk, sugar, salt, beaten eggs and oil. Sprinkle yeast on top of mixture. Do not stir. Set aside for 10 minutes. Then measure flour carefully. Stir 7 level cups of flour into the batter. The dough will be very sticky. Spray large bowl with cooking spray and turn dough into the bowl. Select a linen or "flour sack" dish towel and wet it. Place wet towel on top of bowl and place bowl in a warm spot in your kitchen. Allow dough to rise until double in size.

Turn dough onto well-floured board (use 1/2 cup flour) and divide into four equal parts. Using just a bit of flour, turn and shape dough into four rounds. Allow dough rounds to rise until double in size – about 30 minutes.

Take each round, punch down and roll out into a 10 to 12-inch roll. Twist and flip ends to form a pretzel shape with sides touching one another like a braid – holes disappear as the dough

rises and this is fine. The goal is a more rounded loaf rather than a pretzel with holes. Place on greased cookie sheet (two pretzels per sheet) and allow to rise until double in size – about 20 minutes.

Bake at 375 degree for 15 to 20 minutes until golden brown. While still just slightly warm, frost with vanilla icing (confectioners' sugar, butter and vanilla recipe) and top with shredded coconut or chopped walnuts or pecans.

Note: This light, sweet, yeast bread, shaped like a pretzel and frosted is made in Amana just before New Year's. It's a longtime favorite in the community, having been the New Year's Day treat served in Amana's communal kitchens. Each year, because they are so popular, they are made and sold at our Amana Church Christmas Bazaar.

Yield: four 10 to 12-inch pretzels

Marlene Trumpold

Index